M000211356

the birth of the church
ACTS 1-8

FATH●M

A DEEP DIVE INTO THE STORY OF GOD

FATHOM: THE BIRTH OF THE CHURCH
ACTS 1–8
LEADER GUIDE

Writer: Sara Galyon
Editor: Ben Howard
Designer: Keely Moore

Websites are constantly changing. Although the websites recommended in this resource were checked at the time this unit was developed, we recommend that you double-check all sites to verify that they are still live and that they are still suitable for students before doing the activity.

ISBN: 9781501839320

PACP10510519-01

17 18 19 20 21 22 23 24 25 26 — 10 9 8 7 6 5 4 3 2 1

MANUFACTURED IN THE UNITED STATES OF AMERICA

CONTENTS

About Fathom

Fathom.

It's such a big word. It feels endless and deep. It's the kind of word that feels like it should only be uttered by James Earl Jones with the bass turned all the way up.

Which means it's the perfect word to talk about a God who's infinite and awe-inspiring. It's also the perfect word for a book like the Bible that's filled with miracles and inspiration, but also wrestles with stories of violence and pain and loss.

The mission of *Fathom* is to dive deep into the story of God that we find in the Bible. You'll encounter Scriptures filled with inspiration and encouragement, and you'll also explore passages that are more complicated and challenging.

Each lesson will focus on one passage, but will also launch into the larger context of how God's story is being told through that passage. More importantly, each lesson will explore how God's story is intimately tied to our own stories, and how a God who is beyond our imagination can also be a God who loves us deeply and personally.

We invite you to wrestle with this and more as we dive deep into God's story.

How to Use This Book

First, we want to thank you for teaching this class! While we strive to provide the best material possible for leaders and students, we know that your personal connection with your teens is the most important part of the lesson.

With that out of the way, welcome to the *Fathom Leader Guide*. Each lesson is designed around Kolb's Learning Cycle and moves students through five sections: *Sync, Tour, Reveal, Build,* and *After.*

Sync introduces the students to the general theme of each lesson with a fun activity. There is both a high-energy and low-energy option to choose from in each lesson. *Tour* is the meat of the lesson and focuses intensely on the central Scripture each week. *Reveal* is a time for reflection where youth can digest the information they've heard and start to make to process it. Then the *Build* section puts this newfound knowledge to practice using creative activities and projects. Finally, *After* gives the students options for practices to try throughout the week to reinforce the central concept of the lesson.

Additionally, before each lesson, a Theology and Commentary section is provided to give you a little more information about the topic being discussed that week.

This Leader Guide is designed to be used hand-in-hand with the *Fathom Student Journal.* Each student will need a journal, and the journals should be kept in the class at the end of the lesson. At the end of the study, give the students their journals as a keepsake to remember what they've learned.

Finally, at the end of this book we've included an Explore More section that offers short outlines for additional lessons if you and your class want to keep diving into these Scriptures after the end of this four-week study.

The Fathom 66 Bible Genre Guide

ENTER ZIP OR LOCATION [   ]

Stories TICKETS
★★★★★
Showtimes: Parts of Genesis, Joshua, Judges, Ruth, 1 Samuel,
2 Samuel, 1 Kings, 2 Kings, 1 Chronicles, 2 Chronicles, Ezra,
Nehemiah, Esther, Matthew, Mark, Luke, John, Acts

The Law TICKETS
★★★★★
Showtimes: Parts of Genesis, Exodus, Leviticus, Numbers,
Deuteronomy

Wisdom TICKETS
★★★★★
Showtimes: Job, Some Psalms, Proverbs, Ecclesiastes,
Song of Solomon, Lamentations, James

Psalms TICKETS
★★★★★
Showtimes: Psalms

The Prophets TICKETS
★★★★★
Showtimes: Isaiah, Jeremiah, Ezekiel, Hosea, Joel, Amos, Obadiah,
Jonah, Michah, Nahum, Habakkuk, Zephaniah, Haggai, Zechariah,
Malachi

Letters TICKETS
★★★★★
Showtimes: Romans, 1 Corinthians, 2 Corinthians, Galatians, Ephesians,
Philippians, Colossians, 1 Thessalonians, 2 Thessalonians, 1 Timothy, 2 Timothy,
Titus, Philemon, Hebrews, James, 1 Peter, 2 Peter, 1 John, 2 John, 3 John, Jude

Apocalyptic Writings TICKETS
★★★★★
Showtimes: Daniel, Revelation

The Fathom Bible Storylines

Create 1

Invite I

Act A

Redeem R

Experience E

Hope H

Introduction to The Birth of the Church

Background

Tackling the story of how the church began can be a daunting task. It can appear even more difficult when we consider that the earliest gatherings of Christ-followers, as described in the first chapters of Acts, would not be a "church" in the way we think of that word today. This study comes from the Acts of the Apostles, written by the same author as the Gospel of Luke. Both begin with an address to Theophilus, which means "friend of God" in Greek.

Traditionally, the church is said to begin on the Day of Pentecost, a Jewish festival when people would already be in Jerusalem as a community to celebrate. The coming of the Holy Spirit as described in Acts 2 marks the beginning of a new community made up of followers of Christ who will live together and have their lives forever changed.

As the early church continued to grow after Pentecost, the people had to decide how they would live together. The early chapters in Acts paint a rather idyllic picture of the community in which these early followers lived. Resources were shared, everyone was cared for, and people devoted themselves to learning, praying, and sharing meals together.

However, as any group grows in size, logistical problems are destined to follow. At this point, we begin to see the division of labor amongst the leaders of the church. There were those who preached and baptized, and those who distributed the funds of the church and cared for the widows and the poor.

The road to becoming the church we know today was not an easy one, and in fact it was quite dangerous. Persecution of the early church happened for a variety of reasons, but the central motivation was the threat that Christ-followers posed to the power held by the Jewish leadership. Early leaders of the church were imprisoned, beaten, and killed simply for doing what they knew to be right and preaching the gospel.

For the church to finally become the global communion that we know today, it had to expand beyond its Jewish roots. While Jesus was Jewish himself, he came to minister to those who were both inside and outside of that community, like the Samaritans and the Gentiles. Philip the evangelist continued that work by explaining the gospel to the Ethiopian eunuch, a Gentile who would never previously have been accepted into the Jewish community of believers.

Fathom Strategy for Reading and Understanding the Bible

"The Bible is written for us, but not to us."

This where we start on our quest. When we read the Bible, we have to constantly remember that the Bible is written for us, but not to us. Understanding the original context of the Bible helps us ask the right questions when interpreting Scripture.

For the first steps in our process, we need to understand how each passage we read functions in context and examine the historical background. When we read a passage, we should ask questions about the era, location, and culture of the original audience, as well as how a particular writing relates to the larger narrative of the Bible. This strategy not only helps us understand a passage's primary meaning, it also gives us guidance on how to translate that meaning into our specific circumstances today.

Happy Birthday, Church!

Summary

The church begins with a gathering of people defining what they believe and beginning to learn how to live together. The students will explore how this initial gathering relates to how we gather as believers today.

Overview

- **Sync** with what it might have been like to be part of this early gathering through the concept of either fire or language.
- **Tour** the text of Acts 2:1-41 to figure out how early Christ-followers came to be a community.
- **Reveal** new insights into the text through the practice of lectio divina, and let the students journal about their sensory experience.
- **Build** understanding of how the Holy Spirit is working in the church and in students' lives through an activity that shows how the Spirit is represented in Scripture.
- **After** the lesson, the students will be encouraged to explore different representations of the Holy Spirit throughout the week.

Anchor Point

- Acts 2:4—*They were all filled with the Holy Spirit and began to speak in other languages as the Spirit enabled them to speak.*

Supplies

- Student Journals
- NRSV Bibles
- Clothespins (two to four per student, depending on group size)
- Two black bandannas
- Two red bandannas
- Pens and pencils
- Colored pencils
- Play dough
- Copy paper
- Small prizes

Parent E-mail

This week we begin a new study about the birth of the church. Those we'll be studying in Acts would be better described as followers of Christ than the "church," as that word would not be coined for some time. Some ways you can engage with your student:

- Think about what your core beliefs are. Share them with your student and ask about his or her core beliefs.
- Share how you have experienced the Holy Spirit in your own life and in the life of your congregation.
- Ask your student where she or he sees the Holy Spirit at work.

Leader Notes

How did we become the church? It had to start somewhere, and this week's lesson will give us some insight into how the church as we know it began. This week you'll be taking the students through the Day of Pentecost, and guiding them through the beliefs of the early Christ-followers and exploring the movement of the Holy Spirit through the early community. This week will provide an opportunity to explore how the Holy Spirit is at work in your own community, as well as a chance for the students to explore their own core beliefs.

Theology and Commentary

[Before class this week, read Acts 2:1-42.]

The events that occur on Pentecost mark the beginning of Christianity as we know it. Pentecost was already a tradition celebrated by the Jewish people. The festival would be held fifty days after the beginning of Passover and would last for one week. It was originally intended to be a time of joy and a time to give thanks for the blessing of the harvest. However, by the time of the celebration in Acts 2, it was also viewed as a time to celebrate the giving of the "Law" and the first covenant between God and the Israelites. It's interesting to note that the coming of the Holy Spirit coincides with the people celebrating the original covenant with God.

The scene in Acts 2 begins with all the apostles gathered together. The theme of unity in community will be important throughout the Book of Acts. As they are gathered, they hear a sound like a fierce wind. The word for *wind* in both Greek *(pneuma [breath])* and Hebrew *(ruach)* is the same word that is used for *spirit*. Early readers of this text would have understood that the wind illustrated the coming of the Spirit.

After the wind, individual flames of fire are seen to rest on everyone present. This also would have been understood as a symbol of the divine presence, reminiscent of the time when God appears to the Israelites as a pillar of fire in the wilderness or when Moses encountered God in the burning bush. Fire is also a symbol of purification, like when the Lord makes Isaiah's lips clean by touching them with a burning coal.

Peter's sermon follows, and all of those gathered hear his message in their own languages. This is traditionally viewed as a reversal of the Tower of Babel and a call for people of every tongue to come together and worship Jesus. It could also symbolize a reunification of the Jewish people who had been spread out after the Exile and therefore spoke different languages and dialects.

In his sermon, Peter quotes from Joel 2:28-32. However, Peter makes a few small changes adding phrases like, "in the last days," to emphasize the belief that the kingdom of God had come with Jesus. While this change is not significant, it does highlight how these Scriptures have been interpreted throughout history. Remind your students that they are part of a long lineage of people who are reading Scripture and trying to figure out what it means in their lives.

Peter argues that Jesus is both human and divine, and that not even betrayal and death could overcome the power of God through Jesus. This is showcased in Jesus' victory over death and his resurrection. These assertions became the bedrock of faith for the early followers of Christ, just as they are for our faith today.

Peter uses the testimony of the apostles, who encountered the resurrected Jesus, as well as the miracle of the Holy Spirit that the crowd was experiencing as evidence that what he's saying is true.

In response, the people were moved to ask Peter what to do as followers of Jesus, and he tells them to repent and be baptized for the forgiveness of their sins. Acts 2:41 tells us that about three thousand were baptized that day.

Leader Reflection

There is so much cool stuff going on in this story that it's easy to get caught up in the violent rushing wind and the tongues of fire, and miss the bigger point being made. In his sermon, Peter outlines the central beliefs of the early church: that Jesus was both human and divine, that his death was unjust and undeserved, and that not even death is stronger than the power of God.

What are your central beliefs? What are the things you hold to be true at your core? The students are learning what it means to be part of a community of believers, and sometimes they can get bogged down by the complications of figuring out what to believe for themselves. You can help guide your students by reflecting on your own beliefs and values, like those laid out by Peter at Pentecost.

Take some time before this lesson to think not only about your core beliefs, but how you have experienced the Holy Spirit in your life.

NOTES

SYNC (7-10 minutes)

High-Energy Option—Holy Spirit Clothespin Tag

[Before class, put a pile of clothespins in a corner of the room. There should be two to four clothespins per student. As class begins, gather all of the students in the center of the room.]

SAY: I need two volunteers before we begin. *(If you have a larger class, use four or six volunteers.)*

[Separate these volunteers from the group. Designate half of your volunteers as Apostles by giving them a red bandanna, and half as Opposition by giving them a black bandanna.]

SAY: The rest of you are going to be the early church who has received the awesome gift of . . . clothespins. Well, not really; these clothespins represent the Holy Spirit that the early church received.

SAY: Apostles, your goal is to attach as many clothespins as possible on the members of the early church. Opposition, you are trying to remove those clothespins. The clothespins will stay in their designated area, and only Apostles are allowed to collect them. When I say, "Go," the members of the early church will scatter and try to team up with the Apostles.

[Let the students play for five minutes or so.]

ASK: How did it feel to be the early church? What about the Apostles? the Opposition?

SAY: The early church experienced the coming of the Holy Spirit in a really powerful way, so let's see what Scripture has to say about the Holy Spirit.

Low-Energy Option—Word Jumble

[Before class, either prepare a slide presentation with the following jumbled phrases or write the phrases on pieces of posterboard that the whole class can see. The answers are listed next to the phrases. These are all based on direct or adapted verses from the NRSV Bible.]

1. Bulk Huff Facts—Book of Acts
2. Thus Parrot Like Car Hush In Gwen—The Spirit Like a Rushing Wind
3. Big Ann Twos Be Kin Udder Tongs—Began to Speak in Other Tongues
4. Ton Guess Of Ire—Tongues of Fire
5. Yo Ore Dot Heirs Shell Pro Fit Sigh—Your Daughters Shall Prophesy
6. Penny Caused—Pentecost
7. Cods Deed Soff Pow Her—God's Deeds of Power
8. Gal Ill Eons—Galileans
9. Pee Terse Peaks—Peter Speaks
10. A Poss Lyles—Apostles

SAY: The people gathered for Pentecost spoke many different languages and dialects, but when the Holy Spirit came on to Peter, everyone understood him in their own language. In this game, you will attempt to decipher phrases that won't make sense at first, but after some repetition and some help from Scripture, you'll start to recognize them.

[Write "Olees Parrot" on the board.]

SAY: Who knows what this phrase is? If you're having trouble, say it out loud a few times. That's right; it's Holy Spirit.

[Divide the class into two or three teams, and bring one representative of each team to the front.]

SAY: I'll put one of these jumbled phrases up, and the first person to guess each phrase wins one point for their team. You only get one guess per phrase, and you aren't allowed to look in your Student Journals during this game. Each phrase is associated with our lesson today.

[Play the game, working your way through all the words. Give the winning team a small prize.]

ASK: How many of you found that really difficult? What was it like to hear people speaking gibberish all around you?

SAY: Today we are going to explore a time when a bunch of people gathered together, all speaking different languages, and then miraculously understood each other.

TOUR (15-20 minutes)

ASK: How do you think the church started?

[Even if the students have no idea, encourage them to guess. Wait for a few responses.]

SAY: Today we are going to read about how the early church came to be. This story takes place in the Book of Acts, which is written by the same author as the Book of Luke, and begins right after Jesus has left the disciples and ascended into heaven.

ASK: What do you think it must have been like for the disciples to be without Jesus, now for a second time?

SAY: We're going to focus specifically on the Day of Pentecost. Before we start, does anyone know anything about the Day of Pentecost?

[Pause for answers.]

SAY: Pentecost was a Jewish holiday that began fifty days after Passover. Today we celebrate it fifty days after Easter. It was a time to celebrate the harvest and also a time to celebrate the covenant, or promise, between God and God's people. However, on this particular Pentecost, the people gathered for the celebration are about to experience the beginning of a new covenant with God through Jesus and the coming of the Holy Spirit.

[Split the class into groups of four or five.]

SAY: In your Student Journals, you'll find today's passage. In your group, read this passage together. While you read, underline the parts of it that surprise you and circle the parts that you have any questions about.

[Allow five minutes for groups to read through the passage a few times.]

ASK: In your group, discuss the following questions: What surprised you about this story? What do you think it would feel like to experience the Holy Spirit the way the people gathered on Pentecost did?

[Allow for discussion and then bring the group back together.]

ASK: The disciples were already gathered together when the Holy Spirit came upon them. Why is it important for the Holy Spirit to work through community?

[Allow for responses.]

SAY: A few important things are happening in this passage. First, the Holy Spirit is moving through the people who are gathered, which we'll talk about more in a minute. Second, Peter addresses the crowd and helps them understand what the followers of Christ believe about Jesus being the Messiah. He explains how Christ died, was raised from the dead by God, and how Christ has become more powerful than death.

SAY: This likely sounds familiar because it's still at the core of what we believe as a community today.

REVEAL (10-15 minutes)

SAY: We are going to look back at our Scripture reading again, but in a different way. This time I want you to sit back and listen to the Scripture. You'll hear it twice. The first time, just listen to the words and focus on what you feel when you hear them. What do you think this scene smelled like? What can you hear? What would you see if you were there?

[Read Acts 2:1-42 aloud. If one of your volunteers is a gifted storyteller, have that student read it aloud to the class. Try to make the room as quiet as possible, aside from the reader. After the reading is finished, allow for a minute or two of silence.]

SAY: Now we're going to read this passage again and, this time, you're going to respond to what you sensed during the last reading. You have the option of using play dough, drawing, or writing in your Student Journal as you listen.

[Give everyone a minute to gather the materials you've set out for them to creatively respond. Once they are settled, begin the reading.]

SAY: Share your creative response to the passage with one or two people next to you.

[After the students have had time to share, encourage a few to share with the whole group. Affirm the students' creativity when they share.]

BUILD (10 minutes)

SAY: One of the reasons we responded creatively to God in the last activity is because God is also a creator, and continues to create in our lives even today. God is still active in the world through the same Holy Spirit that worked through the early Christian community.

SAY: Throughout Scripture, the Holy Spirit is described in a number of different ways. You can find them listed in your Student Journal. Using either one of these images or another that springs to mind, I want you to create something that helps describe what the Holy Spirit means to you.

[Make the creative materials from the Reveal section available to the class again. Also, direct them to the creative space provided in their Student Journals.]

SAY: Feel free to use the creative tools we have available to create a sculpture, a drawing, or perhaps a poem that helps explain what the Holy Spirit is to you.

[Give the students seven minutes to create something that represents the Holy Spirit.]

ASK: Would someone please describe what they created? How hard was it to come up with something tangible to represent the Holy Spirit?

[Allow a few students to share.]

AFTER (5 minutes)

[Invite the students to participate in one of the After activities. Send the students a reminder during the week.]

Holy Spirit Photo Challenge

SAY: The Holy Spirit is described in Scripture in many different ways. This week take pictures of what you think represents the Holy Spirit. Share these pictures on social media with *#HolySpiritSightings* so everyone can see what you come up with.

Cut to the Core

SAY: This week talk to your parents about their core beliefs, and share your core beliefs with them. You might be surprised to find out what your parents really believe.

PRAYER

[Ask for student volunteers to help read the following litany, or an adult can read and the students can respond with the phrases in bold.]

LEADER: Awesome God, we thank you for the Day of Pentecost when you poured out your Spirit on those gathered together.

ALL: Pour out your Spirit on us, Lord.

LEADER: Open our eyes to see the places where your Spirit is represented in our world—in the wind, fire, water, and comfort we experience every day.

ALL: Pour out your Spirit on us, Lord.

LEADER: May we remember all that Jesus was, is, and will continue to be, both for those early Christians and for us today.

ALL: Pour out your Spirit on us, Lord.

LEADER: Give us a passion for our faith, like the passion of the disciples gathered for Pentecost.

ALL: Pour out your Spirit on us, Lord.

LEADER: We ask all of these things in your name. **Amen.**

FATH●M
Trouble in the Early Church

Summary

This week the students will examine what it meant to be part of the early church, and how the growth of the church caused problems within that community.

Overview

- **Sync** the students with the tension between individual and communal living through an activity that illustrates the problems each can create.
- **Tour** through several Scripture readings that describe what the early church was like.
- **Reveal** the similarities and differences between the early church and our current community.
- **Build** an understanding of what it means to serve in community through the testimony of a guest speaker.
- **After** the lesson, the students will choose an activity that helps them understand the breadth of community in your church.

Anchor Point

- Acts 2:46-47—*Every day, they met together in the temple and ate in their homes. They shared food with gladness and simplicity. They praised God and demonstrated God's goodness to everyone. The Lord added daily to the community those who were being saved.*

Supplies

- Student Journals
- Small wrapped candies, about five per student
- Two containers
- Index cards
- Pens/pencils
- A volunteer from your church to speak about how he or she was called to service (details in the Build section)

Parent E-mail

Continuing our look at how the church came to be, this week we will be exploring how the early church lived together. While it may seem that the early church is very different from our experience of community today, this week's lesson provides the opportunity to examine how we are sharing in the same body of Christ. Here are some ways you can engage with your student this week:

- Think about how you have been formed by your faith community and how you feel called to participate in it. Share this with your student and ask her or him to consider the same question.
- Discuss ways you see your church living out the ideals of Acts 2:42-47.

Leader Notes

The students may feel very removed from the early church because these first Christ-followers lived so long ago. Helping students work through these passages about the early church, like the division of labor in Acts 6, will help them look at the leadership of their church in a new way. It will also help them understand how your church shares similarities with the early church, even though it existed thousands of years ago.

Theology and Commentary

[Before class this week, read Acts 2:42-47; 4:32-37; and 6:1-7.]

In Acts 2:42-47, we find that the early followers of Christ placed a heavy emphasis on community. The Greek word for *community* is "koinonia," which means more than simply gathering together, but rather is a deep, intimate oneness. Verses 42-47 give us an overview of how this kind of communal life played out in the church.

Another social phenomenon in the early church was the communal ownership of property. Some even sold their possessions so that the proceeds could go into a central account to be distributed as needed. We see this both in Acts 2 and Acts 4. Chapter 4 expands on the idea, saying that there was not a needy person left in the early church as a result of this mutual sharing. This was not a societal norm where they lived.

The dominant social ethic was that the rich stayed rich by exploiting the poor. We see this when Jesus confronts those in religious circles who are not taking care of the poor as they should. Instead of following custom, the church chooses to share with one another, regardless of social station.

The early church also gathered at the temple for worship and prayer. This is probably a reference to the Jewish practice of meeting in the temple for daily prayer. Afterwards, they would share a meal. This isn't Communion in the way we celebrate it, but an actual meal. This communal meal will eventually give rise to some problems in the early church as followers move away from this early idealized version of community and let social norms and ideas creep back into their practices.

In Acts 6, we see some of these early problems. Greek-speaking Jews feel that their widows are not receiving their rightful share of the daily distribution of food. As the church grows in numbers, there is a strain on the organizational structure.

The Greek-speaking followers feel left out by the Hebrew followers. While all of these followers are Jewish, their cultural differences with regards to language and place of origin caused social strife within the group. This particular argument led the apostles to understand that they would need to step in.

From the beginning, the apostles oversaw the care of the needy as well as the preaching of the gospel. This would become more and more challenging as the church grew. The management of distributing resources was likely quite a challenge logistically. In response, the community calls seven men to take on the task of caring for the needy.

This is where we, as the church today, get our modern understanding of the diaconate. Many churches have a separation between clergy who perform the duties of Word and sacrament, and those whose work mimics the service work of the early deacons. In The United Methodist Church, these roles are called Elders and Deacons. For more information about how your church views the role of the diaconate, ask your pastor.

Leader Reflection

Living in community is a messy endeavor, so messy that we don't often think about what it means to live with one another. We isolate ourselves and focus on our families and our work, and treat our Christian community as just one more thing we do during the week.

The early Christians we'll read about this week were living life in a completely different way. They were selling all of their possessions and allowing the proceeds to be distributed to those in need. That's a radical departure from our lives. Despite the differences, however, we still experience community in our own ways. In what ways has your Christian community affected your life?

This week we're also reading about the establishment of the diaconate, also known as those set aside to do the work of service in the community. How do you understand the role of those set aside for that purpose? Do you know who they are in your community? If you don't have specific names for them (i.e. deacon), then think of those in your community who are called to service. Give them a call this week and be sure to pray for them before your lesson.

NOTES

SYNC (10-15 minutes)

High-Energy Option—Rapid Rock, Paper, Scissors

[For this game, you'll need five wrapped candies per student. Before class, write the following life situations on strips of paper or index cards. Make sure you have enough situations for every person in the group to have one. Duplicate situations, if necessary. Place the cards facedown in a container at the front of the room, with an empty container beside it.]

1. My family has two adults with full-time jobs, with health benefits and no debt. (2)
2. My family is behind on all of our bills and won't be able to pay rent this month (3)
3. My family owns a house in a gated community, as well as two vacation homes. (1)
4. My family is on government assistance, and though we work, we can't pay our bills. (4)
5. My family has two kids in college, and one parent just lost their job (3)
6. My family owns our house and both cars, but we live paycheck to paycheck. (2)
7. My family is homeless. (5)
8. I am sick and have no one to visit me. (4)
9. I am a billionaire. (1)
10. I am in prison. (5)

[Distribute five wrapped candies to each student and instruct them not to eat them.]

SAY: We're going to play some rapid-fire games of "Rock, Paper, Scissors." Choose a partner and play a quick round of "Rock, Paper, Scissors." The winner gets to take a candy of their choice from the loser. When you're done, find a new person and play another round. Same rules apply. At the end of five minutes, the person with the most candy wins.

[Start the clock. After one or two minutes, announce the following rule.]

SAY: If you run out of candy, you can keep playing to try and win candy from someone else. No one may refuse to play someone with no candy.

[Continue the game. After five minutes, call time and declare a winner. Make a big deal about how the winner deserves all the candy they won.]

SAY: You all worked hard for your candy, but we're a community here, so I want you to put all your candy here.

[Pick a central location for everyone to place their candy winnings.]

SAY: When you come to put your candy on the table, take a card out of the container then go back to your seat. Even those without candy should come get a card.

SAY: Now I'm going read a life situation. If this situation matches the one you picked, stand up and I'll tell you how many pieces of candy you get to take from the table.

[Work through the list of situations and distribute candy based on the number next to the situation. Mix up the order in which you read the situations. After everyone has taken their turn, ask the following questions.]

ASK: Did anyone end up with no candy after the "Rock, Paper, Scissors" game? How did that feel?

ASK: How did you feel having to give back all of the candy you earned in the game?

ASK: What did you think about how the candy was distributed with the life situations? Was it fair? Why or why not?

Low-Energy Option—Community Resources

[For this activity, you'll need five wrapped candies per student. Before class, write the life situations from the High-Energy Option on strips of paper or index cards.]

SAY: We're going to divide up into groups of five. Each group should gather in a circle.

[Give each student five candies and a life situation card.]

SAY: Each of your small groups represents a community, and communities share, so place your candy in the center of the group. One at a time, go around the group and share the life situation you've been given. After everyone has shared, the group must decide how many pieces of candy each person should receive based on that situation. Write your group's situations and the number of candies you distributed in your Student Journal.

[Give the group five minutes to work together and sort out how much candy each person should receive. Remind them that you will be asking them for their reasons when you gather back together.]

SAY: Let's bring everyone back together. Who wants to share how they distributed the candy?

[Allow a few groups to share. Press them about why they made the decisions they made.]

ASK: What was hard about this activity for your group? Did anyone not have a difficult time dividing up resources? What did this activity make you think about when you think about the way our larger community distributes resources?

TOUR (15-20 minutes)

SAY: Today we are going to take a look at three different passages from the Book of Acts that help us understand how the church began its early life together. Before we start reading, however, what do you think the early followers of Christ did when they gathered together?

[Allow a few minutes for answers. If they struggle with the question, ask follow-ups like, "What do you think worship looked like?" or "What do you think they did outside of worship?"]

SAY: Those are all great answers! Let's dive into the Scripture together and explore what the Book of Acts says about the early church. First, I need you to split into three groups.

[Divide the students into groups, and move them to different areas around the room.]

SAY: Each group will be assigned one of three passages from Acts that can be found in your Student Journal. Your group needs to read the passage and then answer the corresponding questions in your Student Journals. Decide as a group what answers you want to share with the larger group when everyone comes back together.

[Assign each group a passage and give them six to eight minutes to answer their questions.]

SAY: I hope you all learned something about the early church that you might not have known before. Now, I want one member of each group to come up front and share what you discovered through your study of Scripture.

[Allow one member of each group to share what their group's passage was about and their answers to the questions they were assigned. The groups and their questions are listed below.]

Group 1: Acts 2:42-47

• What surprises you about the way the first Christians lived together?
• How would you feel if you were asked to sell everything and give the money to the church, even if you knew the church would make sure you had enough to live on?

Group 2: Acts 4:32-37

• What stood out to you about this passage?
• Are there things you are hesitant to give up for God, like the way Barnabas gave up his field?

Group 3 Acts 6:1-7

• Why do you think certain widows were being neglected?
• How do you feel about the disciples saying that preaching the word was more important than "waiting tables" (or serving the poor)?

REVEAL (10-12 minutes)

SAY: I'm going to give you some time to explore on your own how our worshipping community is similar and also different from the early church.

SAY: In your Student Journals, you'll find a Venn diagram. On the top circle, it says "Early Church," and on the bottom circle it has a blank line where you can write in the name of our church. You've probably used a Venn diagram before, but in case you haven't, the big circles are where you can write facts about the early church and our church that are unique to each community, and the overlapping space in the middle is where you'll place things they have in common. Take the next seven minutes to reflect and fill the diagram.

[Allow the students five to seven minutes to fill out the Venn diagram. If your class has problems with silence, consider playing some worship music quietly in the background.]

ASK: Who wants to share what they wrote? What did you find that was similar? What were the major differences?

SAY: While there are many similarities and many differences between our church and the early church, one thing has always remained the same: We were all called to serve God. You are being called by God to serve here in the same way that the first disciples were called thousands of years ago. If you would like to talk more about how you can serve, please let me *(or one of the other volunteers)* know, and we'll help you figure out how your gifts can best be used to serve God's kingdom.

BUILD (10-15 minutes)

SAY: In Acts 6, we hear about seven people who were chosen to serve God's kingdom. Historically, these people were called "deacons," which is still a word used in the church today for those who are called to service. Today we're going to hear from someone in our faith community who is set apart to serve both in the church and in the world.

[Invite your guest up and have her or him introduce herself or himself.]

SAY: While our guest speaks, I want you to do two things. One, consider what questions you have for this person about the service she or he does. Write these questions in your Student Journal.

[Invite the guest to speak for three to five minutes about how she or he serves in the church and what inspired her or him to do this service.]

ASK: What questions do you have for our speaker?

[Allow time for three to four questions. Thank your speaker for her or his time.]

SAY: In your Student Journal, I want you to draw an outline of a person. In that outline, I want you to write or sketch different things that a person called to serve God could do with his or her brain, heart, hands, mouth, ears, and feet. These instructions are also in your Student Journal. Take the next four minutes to respond.

[Give the students four minutes to write out their ideas.]

ASK: Who wants to share what they've come up with?

[Let as many students share as time allows.]

AFTER (5 minutes)

[Invite the students to participate in one of the After activities this week. Send them a reminder about their choice during the week.]

#AllTheGifts

SAY: This week we learned about ways the early church lived together a long time ago. We still live together as a church today, and it takes a lot of people with a lot of different gifts to carry God's mission into the world. This week post a picture on social media every day that shows one of the people, places, or things that it takes for a church to do life together. Use *#AllTheGifts*.

The Daily Community

SAY: Come and visit the church sometime this week so you can see all of the different people it takes for the church to operate. Record your observations to share with us next week, and take a selfie with some of the people you see working here this week.

[Suggest times that would work best for your church (i.e. choir rehearsals, adult studies, times when volunteers are working, and so forth).]

Family Service

SAY: Talk to someone in your family and ask them how they serve the community. Ask them what they feel they are gifted at and where they would like to serve more. Share with them the gifts you think you have and what you might do with those gifts to serve God.

PRAYER

[Read the following prayer together as a class.]

God of all people, we thank you for those whose hearts are moved to serve others, and for those who share generously of all you have given them. Give us hearts for service and generosity, and help us to seek out those who are in need that we may do your work in our communities here and now, just like the early Christians did so long ago. Amen.

Power and Persecution

Summary

The early followers of Christ faced a number of problems, including persecution from different religious and political authorities. This week we'll learn about this persecution, and the students will explore issues of persecution around the world today and how they can support and pray for those who experience it.

Overview

- **Sync** with the theme of injustice by participating in an activity that illustrates how people can gain power over others.
- **Tour** through stories of persecution in Acts as the students reenact the narratives of the early Christians and learn from each other.
- **Reveal** deeper reflections by reading articles about persecution today and asking the students to journal their thoughts.
- **Build** understanding of how to respond to persecution through a creative group activity.
- **After** the lesson, challenge the students to deepen their understanding of persecution with one of the activity options.

Anchor Point

- Acts 5:27-29—*The apostles were brought before the council where the high priest confronted them: "In no uncertain terms, we demanded that you not teach in this name. And look at you! You have filled Jerusalem with your teaching. And you are determined to hold us responsible for this man's death." Peter and the apostles replied, "We must obey God rather than humans!"*

Supplies

- Student Journals
- News articles about modern-day persecution, one for every two students (more details can be found in the Reveal section)
- Writing utensils
- A small prize(s)

Parent E-mail

This week we are going to explore persecution against Christ's earliest followers, a factor that greatly shaped the early church. The students will learn about how dangerous it would have been to follow Christ during this time, and will also be discussing persecution in the world today. Here are some ways to engage this week:

- Do some research on cases of persecution in the world. Help your child understand these cases and discuss ways you can support people who are under threat of persecution. As a family, pray for these people.
- Share some experiences of injustice that you have witnessed. Describe how you responded or how you wish you had responded differently.

Leader Notes

This lesson may be a bit difficult. Though the concept of persecution may be familiar to your students, it is unlikely that they have dealt with this personally. Push your students to practice empathy and place themselves in the situations of both the persecuted and the persecutors. Also, help them seek out more information about any of the situations covered today if they express additional interest.

Theology and Commentary

[Before class this week, read Acts 5:17-42; 6:8-15; and 7:54–8:3.]

The sections we're using for today's lesson detail various stories of arrest and persecution faced by the early church. It's important to understand the challenges faced by early Christians to understand how those challenges helped form the church.

In Acts 4, Peter and John are arrested while visiting the temple. While it's not a focus in today's study, it bears mention since it establishes a template for these arrests. Peter is arrested after performing a miracle, and the leaders question in whose name he has performed it. When the leaders realize they have no way to punish Peter and John, they send them away and warn them not to continue preaching in the name of Jesus.

The next arrests occur in Acts 5 when the high priests and officials are not only angry, but "overcome with jealousy." The apostles are put in prison, but are set free by an angel who tells them to go to the temple and preach about the Christian life. When the Jerusalem Council learns they have broken out of prison, the Council orders the guards to quietly bring them back to the prison.

When the apostles are questioned after their third arrest, they insist it is more important to obey God than the Council. They also remind the Council again that it was their fault Jesus was killed, and that even though they tried to hold Jesus in contempt with such a humiliating death, God exalts Jesus and holds him at God's right hand.

At this point, the Sadducees want to kill the apostles, however, they are not the leading authority within the Jewish power structure and would need the support of some of the Pharisees. In this case, it is the Pharisee Gamaliel who comes to the aid of the apostles saying that he has seen many false teachers, and if these apostles are in fact false teachers, the people will eventually refuse to follow them. He points out that if they are on the side of God, the Council does not want to fight against God, so it might be better to just let them go.

The Council has the men flogged and releases them, again telling them not to preach in the name of Jesus, an order they immediately ignore.

Acts 6 and 7 detail the arrest and trial of Stephen. Remembering the lesson last week, Stephen is one of those chosen to be set apart for ministry and service. Stephen would preach in the Synagogue of Former Slaves and was arrested after some were enticed to make up claims that he had insulted Moses and God.

In Acts 6:15–7:54, Stephen gives a prophetic sermon detailing the failings of the religious leaders in the Jewish community. These leaders were furious with him, and Stephen is shown a vision of Jesus standing at the right hand of God. When he tells them what he sees, they are further enraged because Jesus standing beside God's throne establishes him as an equal to God. They consider this equivocation blasphemous.

The Council was outraged by Stephen's sermon, and what may have originally been only a punishment (like the flogging and release of Peter and John) escalates quickly into a stoning and the death of Stephen. It is important to note that this is the first time we are introduced to Saul, who will become Paul. Here he is involved in the persecution of the church and has yet to have his conversion experience, but this is a good introduction to Saul's life before his conversion.

Leader Reflection

We hear stories of persecution around the world today or in history books, and we feel like it is very far removed from us. In many ways it is, but that doesn't mean there aren't groups of people in our communities today who are at a disadvantage because of the way they are treated by the powerful in our society. These disadvantages may be subtle or overt, but they exist in every community along lines of race, gender, sexual orientation, and socioeconomic class.

While it is often hard to empathize with those who are not like us, especially if we find ourselves in positions of power, it is something we are called to do as Christians. This week would be a great opportunity to pray for those who experience persecution, both large and small, and to think about how we relate with groups that are marginalized and persecuted.

Who are those around you and around the world that you can be praying for? Who in your community can you stand up for when you see persecution happening?

NOTES

SYNC (10-15 minutes)

High-Energy Option—Relay for Power

[Before class, find an open space, like a gym, parking lot, or open room, that is suitable for a relay race. Make sure it is available when your class meets.]

SAY: To start today, you're going to compete in an event entitled, "Relay for Power." I should warn you upfront, the people who win this relay are going to be rewarded, so I need you to pay attention and follow directions. First, divide up into teams of four.

[Note: If your group is larger, you can make these teams larger or if you have a smaller group, they can have as few as three. Either way, you need between two and four teams total. Also, don't worry about making the teams even.]

SAY: I need all the teams to line up at one end of the race area. Each team member is going to have to get to the other end of the area and back, then tag the next teammate, relay-style, until everyone has gone. However, we have some extra rules:

1) People with blue eyes have to crawl.
2) People taller than 5 foot 3 inches have to hop on one foot.
3) People with brown hair have to walk backward.
4) People who wear glasses or contacts have to roll.
5) If you don't fit in any of these categories, you may run.

[Note: If these categories don't work for your group (i.e. no one has blue eyes or everyone has brown hair), please change them to fit your group.]

SAY: When I say, "Go," the first team member will go. First team to get everyone back wins.

[Begin the race. Make sure everyone keeps to their restrictions. After the race is complete, make a big deal of rewarding the winning team.]

SAY: Thank you all for participating in our race today! Now, I want those who won to stand up. You are now the leaders of this group, and you have the power to make any rules you want for the rest of the class to follow. What rules do you think you'd like to create?

[Give them a few moments to come up with some random rules for the class.]

ASK: To those of you without power, what do you think about this setup? Is it fair that they get to be in control when you were held back by these seemingly random race rules? Isn't this unfair?

[Give the losing team members a few minutes to complain.]

SAY: Power structures created by people are notoriously unfair, and today we are going to read about some of those structures that threatened the safety of the early church in the Book of Acts.

Low-Energy Option—Step Forward, Step Backward

[Before class, make sure you have a reward for the winners—maybe it's best seat in class or a small gift card. Note: You are the expert on your students, so if some of these questions will not affect anyone in the group (i.e. no one has blue eyes), feel free to modify them to fit your group.]

SAY: To begin today, we're going to play a game called, "Step Forward, Step Backward." You should know upfront that the winner of this game is going to be rewarded, so you need to pay attention and follow directions.

[Don't tell the students that winning means getting to the front, or they may not answer honestly.]

SAY: I need everyone to line up in the middle of the room in a straight line, shoulder to shoulder. Take a step forward or backward depending on the following instructions.

1) Step forward if you have blue or green eyes; backward if you have brown eyes.
2) Step forward if your hair is short; backward if it is long.
3) Step forward if you have blond or red hair; backward if you have brown or black hair.
4) Step forward if you are over 5 foot 3 inches; backward if you are under 5 foot 3 inches.
5) Step forward if you are a good singer; backward if you hate to sing.
6) Step forward if you can play an instrument; backward if you cannot.
7) Step forward if you prefer math; backward if you prefer English.
8) Step forward if you prefer basketball; backward if you prefer football.

[Take down the names of students who make it to the front of the group.]

SAY: Okay, we're going to play another round, but the instructions are going to have a bit of a twist. Listen up!

1) If you have never disagreed with the government, step forward; if you have, step back.
2) If you have never argued with a teacher, step forward; if you have, step back.
3) If you feel free to choose your own church, step forward; if you don't, step back.
4) If you think the government supports your religious beliefs, step forward; if not, step back.
5) If you think your church is right about most things, step forward; if you disagree with the church a lot, step back.
6) If most of your friends believe what you believe, step forward; if not, step back.
7) If your parents belong to a different denomination than their parents, step forward; if not, step back.
8) If you feel relatively safe everywhere you go, step forward; if not, step back.

[Record the names of those in the front, and ask everyone to sit down.]

SAY: Thank you all for playing! Now I want those whose names are on this list to stand up. You are now the leaders of this group, and you have the power to make any rules you want for the rest of the class. What rules do you want to create?

[Give them a few moments to come up with some random rules.]

ASK: To those of you without power, what do you think about this setup? Is it fair that they get to be in control when you were held back by these random rules? Isn't this unfair?

[Give the losing team members a few minutes to complain.]

SAY: Power structures created by people are notoriously unfair, and today we are going to read about some of those structures that threatened the safety of the early church in the Book of Acts.

TOUR (20-25 minutes)

SAY: This week we're going to explore three passages from the Book of Acts that show how persecution affected the early church. Persecution is the hostile treatment of people due to something like their race or religion.

SAY: For us to learn about what it meant to be persecuted in the early church, you are going to become the teachers today. We're going to divide into three groups, and I'll assign each group a passage from Acts. Read the passage as a group, then design a short skit based on the passage to show us what happened. Be creative, but respect what Scripture says and don't add things into the story. Rewording dialogue is okay as long as the meaning stays the same. You'll have about ten minutes to plan and three minutes to present it.

[Split the class into three groups. Assign each group one of the following passages: Acts 5:17-42; Acts 6:8-15; Acts 7:54–8:3. This kind of activity can run longer than intended, so be sure to watch the time and have other volunteers help out if possible. After about three minutes, say the following . . .]

SAY: If you're having a hard time with creativity, remember that most of these passages lend themselves to simply being read aloud while the rest of your group acts out the passage.

[Note: If your class is not large enough for three groups, have a group of students/adults prepared to act out the first passage to demonstrate how to do the assignment.]

SAY: All right. Let's all come together and share what we learned with each other.

[Let each group present their skit one at a time. After all the groups have presented, ask the following questions.]

ASK: Did anything surprise you about these passages? What did it mean to be persecuted in the early church? How do you think it felt to be part of a community that was hated by the people in power?

REVEAL (5-10 minutes)

[Before class, gather news articles for the students about persecution, at least one for every two students. You can find articles at www. opendoorsusa.org/christian-persecution and www.christianitytoday. com/ct/topics/p/persecution/. Articles should contain information about who is being persecuted, how it is happening, where it is located, and any other pertinent information to the situations going on in the world around us.]

SAY: I'm going to give you an article that talks about persecution in the world today. Read the article and then reflect on the questions in your Student Journal.

[Pass out the articles and give the students five to seven minutes to write about the questions in their journals.]

ASK: Who wants to share what their article was about and how they responded?

Journal Questions
1. What surprised you about your article?
2. How does your article make you feel about our connection to the early church?
3. Why is it important to discuss persecution when we don't really experience these same things here in the US?

BUILD (15-20 minutes)

SAY: In the United States, it can be difficult for us to understand a concept like persecution. Around the world, however, there are very real cases of persecution happening every day. Can you think of any you've heard recently from the news?

[Allow for a few answers. If they're having problems thinking of any, bring up incidents from the past.]

SAY: I want you to get back into your skit groups from earlier. This time I want your group to come up with a skit that illustrates the kind of persecution you might encounter happening to someone in our society. How will you respond to this kind of injustice? You'll have ten minutes to plan your skit and three minutes to present.

[Give the groups time to plan and present their skits. As they are planning, walk around the room to make sure the skits cover the topic of persecution in an appropriate way.]

SAY: Right now you're at a time in your life when you're learning how to decide what is true and what isn't. That's a hard skill to learn, and lots of adults don't have a handle on it either. Your faith will shape your views on lots of things, including how to address injustice and persecution.

AFTER (5 minutes)

[Invite the students to participate in an After activity. Send them a reminder during the week.]

Everyday Pray

SAY: This week pray for a specific person or group of people who are being persecuted. It could be from the article you read, or it could be someone at your school who you think is treated poorly because of their faith, race, or another reason. Write it down, and pray for them every day. If it helps, consider writing your prayer out every day in a prayer journal.

Worship Scavenger Hunt

SAY: Over the course of this week, take photos of all the different places of worship you can find near where you live, and post them on social media. This will help you illustrate how free we are to worship in the United States since our churches don't have to be hidden from anyone. See how many different religions or denominations you can find!

Over the Generations

SAY: Ask your parents about what they think about issues of oppression and persecution. If you have grandparents or other family members, ask them about stories they may remember from the news when they were growing up.

PRAYER

[Allow for a minute of silent reflection with your class, and then say the following prayer.]

SAY: Wondrous God, we know you ache for those throughout the ages who have suffered for your name. We pray the comfort that only you can provide be upon those in our own time who are suffering at the hands of people who don't know you. Help those in power to show mercy to the faithful and turn their hearts to your love and justice. Move our hearts where you would have them go to show mercy and compassion to those in our own community who suffer because of their race, faith, or beliefs, and embolden us to stand with those who are struggling. Amen.

FATH●M
New Ears to Hear the Good News

Summary

The early church couldn't grow without apostles sharing the good news about Jesus wherever they were called. This week the students will look at the story of Philip and the Ethiopian eunuch, which is a great example of going where God calls and sharing the good news of Jesus.

Overview

- **Sync** with the idea of a connected and expanding community through one of the activity options.
- **Tour** the story of Philip and the Ethiopian eunuch, while discussing some of the important themes of this passage.
- **Reveal** the students' anxieties about sharing the gospel through an activity using journaling and prayer.
- **Build** on the theme of mission work by learning about missionaries from history and creating a talk show to interview them about their lives.
- **After** the lesson, invite the students to participate in one of the activities this week to reinforce how God is calling them to share and serve.

Anchor Point

- Acts 8:36-38—*As they went down the road, they came to some water. The eunuch said, "Look! Water! What would keep me from being baptized?" He ordered that the carriage halt. Both Philip and the eunuch went down to the water, where Philip baptized him.*

Supplies

- Student Journals
- Dominoes (see Sync and After sections for specifics)
- Sharpie markers (silver ones, if your dominoes are black)
- Writing utensils

Parent E-mail

This week we will be reading the story of Philip and the Ethiopian eunuch from Acts chapter 8. This story is all about evangelism and the need to share the good news of Jesus. Here are some ways you can engage your student this week:

- Discuss how you first heard the gospel. The more comfortable teenagers can become talking about matters of faith in their home, the more comfortable they will be sharing their faith with friends and others.
- Talk to your student about a time you've shared the good news of Jesus. How did the situation come up? What did you say? Were you nervous?

Leader Notes

This story may seem straightforward—Philip is called by God to go meet a man and share the good news—but the reality is much more complex. Philip had been sharing the gospel with Samaritans, who were viewed as outsiders, and as a result, the church continued to grow. We need to remind teenagers that sharing the gospel can be as simple as reaching out to someone who they view as an outsider. Encourage them to reach out to those on the margins to show God's love.

Theology and Commentary

[Before class this week, read Acts 8 in its entirety.]

Our story opens up with a man named Philip called by God. The Philip in this story is not the same as Philip the apostle who remained in Jerusalem with the rest of the apostles following the death of Stephen as the rest of the church in Jerusalem scattered.

The Philip in this story is one of the seven men chosen to help care for the widows in Acts 6. In Acts 8, we are told that Philip preached the good news in Samaria. The Samaritan people were historically the result of intermarriage between Israelites and outsiders. While they practiced a form of Judaism, they were seen as neither Jew nor Gentile, and were thus treated like "half-breeds" and people to be avoided. However, we remember from the Gospels that Jesus both cared for Samaritans (the woman at the well in John 4:1-26) and used them as positive examples in his parables (the good Samaritan in Luke 10:25-37).

Following what seems to be a successful ministry in Samaria, our passage today begins with Philip being called by an angel to take the desert road that runs from Jerusalem to Gaza. While this seems fairly straightforward, one has to understand that there was plenty of work for Philip in Samaria, and to travel through the desert would mean uncertainty for Philip. Travel in the first century was difficult, but Philip trusts God and goes where he is sent.

On the road, he encounters the Ethiopian eunuch's carriage. The basic definition of a eunuch is a castrated man, and most were employed to guard women's living areas in courts and palaces. This particular eunuch was in the employ of the Queen of Ethiopia, and was a court official. He was a man of great dignity and was in charge of the queen's treasury.

He is also assumed to be a proselyte (convert to Judaism) or a "God-fearer," which was a Gentile who worshipped God, but hadn't converted. Scripture says he had gone to Jerusalem to worship and was heading home.

Eunuchs were forbidden from entering the inner court of the temple for worship, so this man would have been restricted to the court of the Gentiles, where the unclean and outcasts were made to gather. God's decision to have Philip preach to this man signifies the expansion of the Kingdom beyond the scope of Jerusalem and Samaria to those historically restricted from entering further into the temple.

When Philip approaches the carriage, he hears the eunuch reading from the prophet Isaiah. Some see this story as a fulfillment of the passage in Isaiah 56:3-5 which says:

"Don't let the immigrant who has joined with the LORD say, 'The LORD will exclude me from the people.' And don't let the eunuch say, 'I'm just a dry tree.' The LORD says: To the eunuchs who keep my sabbaths, choose what I desire, and remain loyal to my covenant. In my temple and courts, I will give them a monument and a name better than sons and daughters. I will give them an enduring name that won't be removed.' "

During this passage, however, the eunuch is reading from Isaiah 53, the last of Isaiah's servant songs. Isaiah 53:7-8 focuses on the unjust death of a servant of the Lord. Philip asks the eunuch if he understands what he is reading, and the man responds that he needs some help to interpret the Scripture.

Philip makes the connection between Isaiah's suffering servant and Jesus. We have no way of knowing if this man had ever heard of Jesus before this encounter, but he comes to faith quickly and asks to be baptized in water they come upon along their journey.

The story ends with Philip being taken by the Spirit and appearing in a town further north, while the eunuch rejoices and returns to his homeland. Ethiopian tradition holds that this is the beginning of the church in Ethiopia, and that this man returned and evangelized to others in his country. This brings to mind the promise in Acts 2:39 that, "The promise is for you, your children, and for all who are far away."

Leader Reflection

How comfortable are you sharing the gospel with others? Since you've taken on the task of working with teenagers, one could guess that, at the very least, you have a basic desire to spread the good news. But the task can be daunting. Some people have an innate gift for sharing the gospel with others verbally, and others do so through service. We need to remember, however, that service by itself is no different than the service of a civic club or other religious group. Sharing the gospel means serving God's kingdom, and at some point, telling others about our faith, our God, and our Savior.

This week take stock about the challenges and insecurities you have about sharing your faith. Who do you struggle to reach out to? Do you have trouble deciding how or what to share? The more comfortable you are with your own struggles, the easier it will be for you to work with your students as they diagnose their own struggles. It is important for them to know that adults struggle with the same things they do. You can be the positive example that lets them acknowledge where they still need to work, without feeling ashamed or disappointed in themselves.

NOTES

SYNC (10-15 minutes)

High-Energy Option—Squiggle Line Tag

SAY: I need everyone to circle up, and I need a volunteer to be "IT." When the game starts, you'll play it just like regular tag. However, when the first person is tagged, they will link arms with the person who tagged them and work as a team. From this point on, whenever someone is tagged, they will join arms with the person who tagged them. Only people on the ends can tag others. The game ends when everyone is part of the line.

[Play as many rounds with your group as time allows. If for some reason the line breaks, simply have the students rejoin and continue.]

SAY: All right. Let's come back together and talk about what that game meant.

ASK: For those of you who were IT first, how did it feel knowing you would eventually have to work to tag everyone?

ASK: When you were on an end, how hard was it to tag people and still remain part of the group? Was it easier when there were only two or three people in the line or when there were more people in the line?

ASK: When you were in the middle of the line, did it ever feel like you didn't really have to do anything but go with the flow of the rest of the line?

SAY: This game illustrates how one person becomes enveloped into the larger group. Sometimes it can be easy to assume that someone else will do the hard work of sharing the good news of Jesus with others, but today we are going to read about a man named Philip who went where God told him to go and shared the good news with a stranger.

Low-Energy Option—Domino Challenge

[Before class, gather as many dominoes as you can for your group. You'll need about one hundred dominoes for every group of four or five students.]

SAY: To start today, we're going to divide into groups of four or five. Each group will get about one hundred dominoes, and with your group, I want you to make the coolest domino course you can imagine. You can use other props to aid your course, but all the dominoes need to fall in sequence after the first domino is tipped over. You can't aid the course in any way.

[Give the groups about seven to eight minutes to design their domino courses. When the groups are done, go through group by group and let them demonstrate whether their course works.]

ASK: What did you find challenging about this activity? What frustrated you about it? What would you do differently if you had to do this activity again?

SAY: Today we are talking about how people were converted to Christianity early in the life of the church. We're going to explore the story of Philip, a man who simply went where God called him to share the good news of Jesus. Not unlike these dominoes, one person hears the good news, then shares it with another, who shares it with another, and the gospel of Jesus Christ is spread all around the world.

TOUR (15-20 minutes)

SAY: How many of you remember our class two weeks ago when we talked about the seven being chosen to assist the apostles?

[Allow time for responses. If no one remembers, help jog their memory using the lesson from two weeks prior.]

SAY: Today's passage focuses on the story of one of those seven men, a man named Philip. Philip is referred to as Philip the evangelist. Can anyone tell me what it means to be an evangelist?

[Evangelist—a person who seeks to convert others to the Christian faith, especially by public preaching. Affirm correct responses and fill in any gaps in student responses.]

SAY: After the death of Stephen in Acts 7, the church was subjected to vicious harassment and began to scatter away from Jerusalem. Philip began to spread the good news throughout Samaria. Has anyone heard of Samaria before?

[Allow for responses. If responses are slow, prompt them to recall the story of the good Samaritan in Luke 10 and the woman Jesus met at the well in John 4.]

SAY: The ancestors of the Samaritans had been Jewish, but intermarried with people from other faiths. Many of them worshipped in a similar manner to the Jewish people, but they were looked down upon by many in the Jewish community. However, Philip goes to Samaria and converts many of the Samaritans by sharing the good news about Jesus. He baptized them, and the church continued to grow. Today's story takes place after Philip has been working in Samaria for some time. I need a volunteer to read the first part of our passage today.

[Have the volunteer read Acts 8:26-29.]

SAY: I want to stop here and take a look at what we just read. An angel tells Philip to take a road through the desert that leads to Gaza. We might not think anything about this, but this is dangerous. Philip is relatively safe in Samaria. He has opportunities for work, food, and shelter. Traveling through the desert without knowing the reason why would be difficult, in addition to being dangerous. But Philip goes because God calls him to go.

[It's possible that the students will have questions about what it means to be a eunuch. A eunuch was a man, typically a slave or servant, who had been castrated in order to serve a particular function. In the case of the Ethiopian eunuch, this was likely because he was a guardian and companion of the queen. This is an easy part of the story to get distracted by, so try and be as straightforward about it as possible.]

SAY: Then he comes upon this Ethiopian man who works for the queen. We can assume that this man is either a Jewish convert or someone who worships the God of Israel because the passage tells us he went to Jerusalem to worship. Because he's a eunuch, however, he would not have been allowed all the way inside the temple. He would have had to stay in the outer court reserved for the unclean and the outcasts. I need another volunteer to read the rest of the story.

[Have the volunteer read Acts 8:30-40.]

SAY: So, Philip is called to leave the security of his life in Samaria and preach the good news to an outsider, someone who isn't even allowed into the inner court of the temple. Not only does he do it, but the man he preaches to comes to believe in Jesus and gets baptized during their journey in some water on the side of the road.

ASK: When you hear this story, why do you think it's included in the Bible? Remember, this is the first story after the death of Stephen. It's one of the earliest stories of the Christian Church. Why is this story so important?

[Allow for responses. Push the students to hone their responses by asking them, "Are you sure?" after they respond.]

SAY: God doesn't just call us to share the good news of Jesus Christ; God calls us to share that good news with everyone, including people who we would never think to talk to. That can be really difficult, but it's what we are called to do.

ASK: What are some insecurities you have about sharing the good news with others?

[Allow for the students to respond to this question in anticipation of the next activity.]

REVEAL (5-10 minutes)

SAY: Spend the next few minutes writing a prayer in your Student Journal about ways you could share the gospel. There are some guiding questions in your journal that may help you as you think things through while you are writing your prayer. Remember, it doesn't need to be perfect, just sketch out something honest.

[Allow between five to seven minutes for the students to write their prayers in their Student Journals.]

Journal Questions
1. What scares you about sharing the gospel?
2. What excites you about the good news of Jesus?
3. Who are you worried about sharing the gospel with?
4. What do you feel like you need more of in order to be bold in sharing Jesus with others?

SAY: I want you to get into small groups of two or three, and share your prayers with each other. If you're not comfortable sharing, you don't have to share. After your group has shared, pray one or more of your prayers together so that we can pray for each others' needs as well as for our own.

BUILD (10-15 minutes)

SAY: Now it's your turn to teach the rest of us about some missionaries and missionary groups that have spread the gospel throughout history. In your Student Journal, you'll find three profiles of people who did missionary work. You are going to work with a group to create a talk show-style interview of the person being profiled.

[Split the class into three groups, and assign each group one of the profiles.]

SAY: If you need more information about your subject, feel free to use your phones or tablets to do additional research. Your Student Journals will also include some guiding questions to help you plan your interview. Your interview should last for three minutes or less.

[Give the groups about eight minutes to put together their short interview skits. Have each group come up and present what they've learned in their skit.]

ASK: Were you surprised by anything that you learned in any of the three skits? Why did it surprise you?

AFTER (5 minutes)

[Invite the students to participate in an After activity. Send them a reminder during the week.]

The Good News of Dominoes

SAY: The good news of Jesus is a lot like a domino course. When someone shares the good news, it can get shared over and over again down the line. This week take one of the dominoes we used earlier and write on the back the name of someone who needs to hear the good news of Jesus this week. Over the course of this week, pray for this person and try to find time to share the good news with him or her.

Called to Serve

SAY: This week share photos of places in your neighborhood or even around the world where you feel called by God to serve. Pray for each of these areas, and if you find an opportunity in your neighborhood, consider volunteering there.

The Family That Shares

SAY: Talk to your family about how they think we should share the gospel with others. How do they share the good news with their friends? with extended family? with neighbors? What could you do as a family to share the good news of Jesus?

PRAYER

SAY: Let's all say the following prayer together.

God of all nations, we pray that you can relieve our insecurities and make us bold to share the good news of Jesus. We pray for all of the missionaries who are following your call in their lives and ask for your guidance in following your will in our own. Amen.

Explore More

Another Is Chosen

Anchor Point
• Acts 1:12-26

Summary

The apostles choose Matthias to replace Judas within the group of Twelve. However, Matthias is never mentioned again after this account, and Paul becomes the obvious peer of the apostles. Use this lesson to understand that sometimes patience is necessary to discern what God intends for us.

Takeaways

• Sometimes we need to wait in order to discern what God intends for us to do.
• Discernment is the art of knowing when to wait and when to act.

Holding Back

Anchor Point
• Acts 5:1-11

Summary

While the followers of Christ shared everything with one another, some apparently weren't ready to go all in. In the story of Ananias and Sapphira, we learn about the consequences of lying, not only to your brothers and sisters, but also to God.

Takeaways

• God requires everything from us, not just the parts we can easily give to God, but the things that are more difficult to surrender.
• Ananias and Sapphira aren't punished because they didn't give all the money; they are punished for lying to the community, and God, about it.

FATH●M

A deeper dive into understanding the key themes and storylines of the Bible.

Continue Your Journey Into God's Story With
The Following Fathom Titles

The Bible
Where it came from and how to read it

The Beginnings
Genesis

The Passion
The Death and Resurrection of Jesus

The Wilderness
Exodus-Deuteronomy

The Coming of Jesus
The Birth of a Savior

The Birth of the Church
Acts 1-8

The Teachings of Jesus
Matthew-John

The Promised Land
Joshua-Judges

The Life in the Church 1
Romans-Philemon

The Life in the Church 2
Hebrews-Jude

The Birth of the Kingdom
From Saul to Solomon

The Wisdom of the Kingdom
Job – Song of Songs

The Spread of the Church
Acts 9-28

The Broken Kingdom
The Fall of Israel

The Leaders of the Church
Profiles in the New Testament

The Exile and Return
Ezra-Esther and the Minor Prophets

The Promise of the Future
Stories of Hope in Ruth, Isaiah & Micah

The Return of Jesus
Revelation

To learn more about all 18 Studies go to
YouthMinistryPartners.com/Studies/Fathom

CPSIA information can be obtained
at www.ICGtesting.com
Printed in the USA
LVOW13s0951140817
544165LV00001BA/2/P

9 781501 839320